The Great Mother Speaks

Linda Heller & Claudia Mardel

BALBOA.
PRESS
A DIVISION OF HAY HOUSE

Balboa Press books may be ordered through booksellers or by contacting:

Balboa Press
A Division of Hay House
1663 Liberty Drive
Bloomington, IN 47403
www.balboapress.com
1 (877) 407-4847

Because of the dynamic nature of the Internet, any web addresses or
links contained in this book may have changed since publication and
may no longer be valid. The views expressed in this work are solely those
of the authors and do not necessarily reflect the views of the publisher,
and the publisher hereby disclaims any responsibility for them.

The authors of this book do not dispense medical advice or prescribe the use
of any technique as a form of treatment for physical, emotional, or medical
problems without the advice of a physician, either directly or indirectly. The
intent of the authors is only to offer information of a general nature to help
you in your quest for emotional and spiritual well-being. In the event you use
any of the information in this book for yourself, which is your constitutional
right, the authors and the publisher assume no responsibility for your actions.

Print information available on the last page.

ISBN: 978-1-5043-5845-3 (sc)
ISBN: 978-1-5043-5846-0 (e)

Library of Congress Control Number: 2016908721

Balboa Press rev. date: 06/21/2016

Dedication

The Great Mother Speaks is dedicated to the Great Mother Herself and to all of Creation so that we may listen and take responsibility for our choices and actions. So that we can choose to create a most beautiful world that our future generations shall enjoy and find in perfect harmony, abundance and beauty.

Dedication

Contents

Foreword

By Ivonne Delaflor A.

Motherhood: All love begins and ends there.
— Robert Browning

When I was invited to write a foreword for this book, I knew there was something different about this experience.

As an author myself, I could feel that this invitation that seemed to be writing a few lines for what appeared to be a book, was actually a call from the Voice of the Great Mother herself for me to receive her love.

This book, beautifully written through the pen of intention and the ink of the soul by authors and spiritual teachers Claudia Mardel and Linda Heller, is a portal, a temple and an altar where the reader can walk through its pages as though walking a sacred forest or place in nature.

Each word shared in this book is a blessing for the soul whose mind is still and whose heart is open.

Each message is a reminder, an embrace, and a warmth whisper of the soul of the great spirit of the feminine energy that nurtures creation in us and without us every given moment.

The Great Mother uses words to remind the seeker, the lovers and all beings that we are capable, beyond belief, of living a life of greatness when we assume the responsibility of our choices.

Her many voices as nature, as elementals and as other beings, seem to call forth our cells to awaken into the divine blue print essence of her love.

This book is a blessing, a timely call, and an invitation to enter the realm of silence and LISTEN.

As we read, our intuition deepens, our love for self and all evolves and our respect for nature grows.

With this book we are presented with a powerful gift; a call to action to our spirit to rise above all fragmented beliefs, and take ownership of its creation, remain humble in its growth, and awaken even higher and deeper into the awakened conscious gift that the sacred Mother wants us all to receive.

All you need to do to receive the blessings is read mindfully,

Settle in the place of sacred stillness, and allow the transmission of this book to soothe your emotional wounds,

To hold you in its arms of grace,

And to whisper in the ears of your heart the voices that the Mother wishes you to hear to rise as the divine child and guardian of humanity that you are.

Voices of the Great Mother is a gift,

Is a song for the soul,

Is the voice of the collective consciousness,

Ready to speak its words of love.

I wish you a great journey, dear reader.

I wish you to experience the great love from The Voices of the Sacred Mother.

Namaste,

Ivonne Delaflor Alexander
Vice President
Brilliant Futures Institute
Creator of the Transcendental Rebirthing System
Author of; The Divine Mother.

Preface

We were inspired to give the Great Mother a voice and let Her tell us what it is that She desires us to know. What is important for Her to pass on to us, so we can make better choices for ourselves and our future generations. We desired to connect to the deep part within ourselves that is not clouded by political views or profit thinking but rather comes from the voice deep within ourselves or around us, available to all of us, when we become silent and listen.

The Voices of The Great Mother Speaks is timeless and not attached to any religion or philosophy. She touches on the wisdom and knowledge that many of the Ancient tribes knew and still preserve to this day. Knowledge that lies in the observance of nature and the humility and respect, that is required for all of creation and Her beings. The Voices of the Great Mother Speaks is birthed from the understanding that we are all ONE: The understanding, that we cannot live without each other, without perfect balance and harmony. Her voice gives us the humility, humbleness and respect that motivate us to take care of Her in the most caring, nurturing way so that, in return, She may take care of us.

This book was and is inspired by Grandfather Bear Eagle with the request for us to bring forth The Great Mother Speaks.

Aho! To All My Relations.

Introduction

This creation has two faces: poetic and pragmatic. It arises out of a very sacred and powerful process: Living in the Question[1]. As we joined to create this offering we had many discussions about how to proceed and what was the highest priority to share.

This offering was birthed from the very basic question: If the Earth, The Great Mother, by whatever name you choose to call her, had a voice what would she share? For many days we surrendered to the question and then, in one moment, it began to unfold. The framework for the voices of the Earth emerged fully formed. What was shown was that she had many voices: Each one was given a place.

In the spirit of collaboration and partnership, we decided to each ask The Great Mother what is it you desire us to hear? For each chapter, what you will read and what you will hear is one voice, with two messages received and shared by two individual messengers. It was very clear to us both, that as the messengers, who wrote which message was not important. So you will find, that in each chapter, each sharing, it is indicated which voice is speaking, it does not indicate who the messenger is.

As we entered into each chapter and asked for the voice to share its message it became clear that something more was being called forth.

The offering evolved two very distinct sections. Part I is the messages, shared by the voices of the Earth. Part II - is a Call to Action. A very pragmatic and practical invitation to step up, make a choice and take one or more individual steps to support the Earth, to create the change you desire to see in the world. These choices are completely dependent upon you the reader. They are doable, replicable and easy. They involve making a conscious choice to create change by how you choose to direct your energetic resources or money.

We are honored that you have chosen to read and listen to the Voices of the Great Mother. It is our prayer that you have the eyes to see, the ears to hear and the heart to feel. That her messages will speak to you, that you will hear her call, and choose - To Make a Change.

The Great Mother Speaks

I AM the Great Mother who came before anything else existed. From my womb was created the world, the Universe, the web that connects everything. Like the thread of the web that never lets go of all who are born into the world, each living being, each mineral and plant, each atom and proton and enzyme, the connections of planets, the connection of stardust held together with the finest glue. It matters not so much your belief system, your conviction, or religion, as it matters for each of you to realize that the connection from me to you and you to me and each of you to everyone and everything affects everything: Literally everything. From the Manifest to the Un-manifest, that which is visible to that which is invisible, from that which has been thought to that which has not been thought yet.

Much has been written about the interconnectedness of this world and yet separation still exists. Divided by the color of your skin, by the thoughts you believe, by the labels you fight for, by the class or gender you think you belong to. When you take a breath and feel the expansion and contraction in your lungs and go within, know that all living beings breathe, breathe the same air as you do and feel the connection from the breath, the inhale and exhale, the expansion and contraction.

Read, listen to my voices and hear my call to action.

PART 1

The Sacred Mother

A Portal has been created

A portal that has never existed before
Enter the gates disguised as pages.

With reverence
Enter and read the words,
words that are not read by the eyes alone.

Words that are
Expressed by the soul of infinite sacred spirit
to your soul.

Enter the field

Be the field

Awaken the Sacred Mother

Sri Yukteswar

Chapter 1

The Voice of Silence

Listen, Oh Children!

You hear the sound of all that is, of all that was, of all that will be. Be still! Know that I Am God. God is in the silence, God will always hear what your heart is speaking, without words. Take a deep breath, listen! What do you hear? The crickets, the birds, the wind, cars going by, an airplane overhead: Perhaps sirens, perhaps a clock, maybe the barking of a dog?

In between all these noises is a hidden pearl. Can you find it? It is the silence. This silence is so vast you can be swallowed up by it. Or, you can choose to become the silence. Pray, meditate, be still: Listen. Pause. Find the gap.

As you read these words - slow down, become silent and listen to your breath and the rhythm of your heart. Can you hear it? Let go, breathe again. Keep listening, without effort. Like a doctor who listens to find out what is going on with their patient beyond what the words of the patient are trying to explain.

It is the same with the vast silence, the breath of the Universe, the Mind of God. What do you hear? Concentrate not on the hustle and bustle of the busy streets, or the children crying and laughing, let it become your background sound. That which you have overheard does not matter, it can fall away.

Silence that matters is more than a hushing up, a being quiet and not speaking. It is much vaster. You become it. Your every cell in your body becomes silence, ready to receive. Receive what, you ask.

Before we speak about receiving let us get there – to the silence. Do not rush into the next step, into the next "what is in it for me", into the next experience to be enjoyed, into the next pleasure to be sought.

Take another breath and look around you. What do you see? Can you see the emptiness among all the things that you are surrounded by? Books on the shelf – they have accumulated dust, your mind exclaims! A coffee cup that is half full – or half empty. Your mind argues, depending on if you are an optimist or a pessimist: Piles of letters, piles of clothes, things on the desk, things that haven't been cleaned up and organized. Maybe I should do this now, your mind suggests, before you ask me to go any deeper into the silence.

Slowly, you can feel your mind surrender. Slowly you can feel yourself coming to yourself, coming into yourself. The busy life around you that you know only too well and have accepted the lists of things to do, people to call back, to write your blog and so forth. The busy life is disappearing, and you bathe in the feeling of grounded-ness and the silence that surrounds you is feeling more comfortable.

There, you find the gap:

A glimpse. Once you've caught a glimpse, it becomes easier as you know what you are looking for. You sit in the garden under a tree and there is a shift in the wind. There is a shift in how the blades of grass move in front of your eyes, how your body feels the sweetness of existence. Time slows down and becomes brighter and lighter, effortless, full of fragrance. It is as if someone put a blanket around your shoulders and you sink into the comfort of silence.

You might become the observer of your mind and watch the chatter dissipate as you expand into the vastness of silence. Once there you feel one with all that surrounds you, with all that is, with the vast space of the Universe, with the sounds and the breath of Mother Earth.

You have come to know me - The Voice of Silence.

The Voice of Silence

I teem with voices.
Yet you who listen do not hear me

I wear many "costumes"
Yet you who visit, never see me.

I come in many colors and textures,
Yet to you, who behold me, I am invisible.

My voice echoes
Through every plant,
Every grain of sand,
And every drop of water.

Yet, how many of you
Truly hear me?
My voice,
Beyond and below
The colors, the sounds, the textures that you experience.

Still your thoughts,
Open your senses even more.

Breathe

In that pause
Between the inhale and the exhale

In that moment of stillness
Open to me.

I am the space that welcomes the song of the birds.
I am the emptiness that welcomes the sound of the wind through
the trees.

I am the space between the worlds as the night completes and the day begins.

I am the roots of plants anchoring into the soil, drawing life giving water and nutrients.

I am the cells of your body.

In that sacred pause - open to me.

Chapter 2

Voice of the Waters

My presence is everywhere, in everything. I am both visible, and invisible. Of all the elements, I am the only one, yes the only one that can occupy 3 states of being in this 3D world.

I am hard and cold, literally frozen in time. You may see me as snow, as ice, you may find me captured in my liquid essence inside of a crystal.

I am invisible – yes, as water vapor you can feel me, yet I am invisible to the naked eye, until, like a shape shifter, I coalesce upon a window pane, the windshield of your car, the mirror in your bath.

And then there is the form where you worship, curse, fear and pray for me. As Rain I fall, sometimes gently, like a lover's soft kiss, sometimes, in torrents so heavy, I steal from you the power of sight. Sometimes accompanied by my sister the Wind, together as a hurricane, in our most extreme form, we invoke fear.

I also come in my other form, as the great lakes of salt water, as the inland seas, as water cool and clear bubbling up from under the protective armor of earth. I am the vast oceans that beckoned your explorers; that provided ever shifting highways for commerce and war and hunting.

Yes, I have many faces, many voices. Sometimes I whisper to you gentle as the soft tendrils of mist floating on the invisible currents of my sister Wind. Sometimes I am the life giver: A drink of water in the vastness of the dessert, needed rain for your struggling crops. Sometimes I am the destroyer, not the life giver.

I am ever changeable, ever present. You are so ignorant in your pursuit of riches and uses of technology. You believe the getting is what is important. You think you can own me.

The ancient tribes knew my value. They appreciated me and my life giving presence. They accepted me as I offered myself, they did not try to capture me, divert my course, or change my nature.

Sometimes there seems to be an abundance of me, sometimes it seems as if I have forgotten you. I am going to share a secret. Did you know that for all of my mutability, for all of my variety of form; There has since the beginning, been only me, in my same quantity, for millions of years, there has never been more, nor less of me. I change forms; I change where I visit my life giving waters. I change in whether I am acidic or alkaline, however my children, there is only this finite amount of me.

Lately it seems that you are treating me like an endless ever renewable resource. You cut down the forests that filter the water so that it returns to the stream, the lake, the ocean clear and pure. You block my path thinking to hold me and save me for a "rainy day". You drain my hidden underground lakes with no thought to the gentle and gradual accumulation of water through millions of years these hidden lakes represent.

What are you thinking? Where are your priorities? You can live without oil pumped through fracking. You can live without gold washed from the mountain sides with pure water pumped from rivers and streams in great quantities. You allow my rivers and streams and lakes to become polluted so that my life giving essence cannot be taken in.

Will I always be here, as I have been before?

I do not know.

Voice of the Waters

Water, holy sacrament,
Bless us and bestow upon us
Eternal life.

Water, source of all Life
Cleanse us and nourish us.
Wash away all sorrows
So we may regain a state of perfect health.

Water, binding piece on Earth
And In the Heavens,
Rain upon us, so we may grow
And nourish others.

Water, symbol of life
Which continues to flow
Through time and space
Preserving generation after generation:
Bless us so our future generations may live
And flourish here on Earth.

Water in your many forms,
Of rain and snow,
Rivers and lakes,
Springs and wells,
All flow into the One Great Ocean
Which represents the
Great Mother Who Speaks.

Water, an expression of all there is.
The Holiest of Holy
Without it no life could exist.

Treat her well and with Reverence
Appreciation and Love
That she may in return nourish your bodies, minds and souls.

Water, in its most subtle form is filled
With oxygen and transports pure
Beings of Air.
Spirits that you have yet to discover
That represent God with each particle
And have always been there
Speaking to all of life in the purest form
Of God Creation

Water: the cycle of all Life
Begins and ends with Water.
All ancient cultures, religions, tribes and seers
Have known this throughout Time.
Recover the sacred knowledge
And experience:

Water. Invaluable. Abundant. Precious.
Sign of life.

Chapter 3

The Voice of the Mineral World

I wonder, is it possible for you to truly hear me? You are so distracted by some of my brothers and sisters: Gold, soft and luminous and warm; never tarnishing, eternal in its beauty and luster and light giving. Silver, also luminous, she however loses her luminosity without ever vigilant care. My sister gems, my brothers iron and coal, my timid relations grains of sand and my massive father and uncles the mountains. I come in so many forms; you say you know, because they are visible to you. You can see my nature, my value, my existence.

Other aspects of my voice are much more silent and invisible. I am the chemicals that keep your heart functioning, your mind organizing and thinking, your bones strong, your muscles and ligaments flexible and strong. You absolutely require my presence in your life. I am the unappreciated necessity.

I am the majestic backdrop for your play time with family and friends. I hold the micro compounds that are necessary for you computers, your cell phones. I am irreplaceable.

You need me.

I however do not require you, for my continued existence. I measure the passage of time so slowly as to be infinitesimal. I can change my form literally in an instant, yet, I have withstood the elements for millions of years. I bear silent witness to the changes upon the Mother.

She keeps giving, you keep taking.

She keeps forgiving; you keep complaining there is not enough

I am the voice of the witness

and I say unto thee

"Be mindful, be grateful".

Take less, care more,

lest the Mother chose to no longer forgive,

to no longer provide.

Heed my words:

take less and care more

Voice of the Mineral Kingdom

The essence of life within
Is ruled by minerals that you need
To live in a healthy body.
Each imbued with a different vibration
And frequency

Too much of anything is not a good thing,
In balance the world becomes free.

Frequency attracts alike.
Each individual mineral has its own frequency and
Can be used for healing specific illnesses
Of the mind and body,
Strengthen or aid in balancing,
Give access to knowledge stored for millennia
In one crystal or rock.

Even more powerful is
A combination of minerals, crystals or rocks.
As the mineral kingdom like all other families
Works in unison and is operating
Under the principle:
Where two or more are gathered in my name...

Minerals, crystals and rocks
Come from an ancient civilization with
Their own missions,
Their own blessings,
Their own higher consciousness.
They are here to serve and protect
And come in groupings and families.

Confusion transforms into clarity
Illness into health
Weakness into Strength
Worry into protection
And questions into knowledge
Under the influence of the mineral kingdom
And crystals and rocks

One of my many voices,
I safe guard them as my children on this
Planet Earth

I am the Great Mother
Who Speaks

Chapter 4

The Voice of Plants

My world, the world of plants has a voice that is a symphony, of diversity. We exist everywhere. We are the tiny algae in the waters. We are the seaweed dancing gracefully in response to the invisible ebb and flow of the ocean currents. We are ancient and brand new. We are the bristlecone pine and the young seedling a harbinger of spring and the promise of the harvest to come.

Without us, there would be no animals, no humans. We are necessary for nourishment, for the very air you breathe, for the fruit that ripens on your trees, the food that sustains you and the animals. We provide health in the form of medicines and tonics and remedies. We give beauty through our form, our color and our fragrance.

You see us, yet - do you hear us? You need us, yet do you protect and value us? Have you become so taken in your own accomplishments that you have forgotten the place that we have in your continued existence?

Truly it is not about you, as much as you desire to think it. We remind you of the interdependent web of life that this earth is. We are the voice of patience, we are the voice of "to everything there is a season", we are the voice that reminds you, cycles end and cycles begin. Truly hear us, and you hear our voice whispering the secret of legacy, of everlasting life, truly hear us and find the voice of brilliance, optimism, the voice of fearlessness and the voice of eternity.

Our voice carries the wisdom to heal, the wisdom of how to live gently, the wisdom of interconnectedness, the wisdom of interdependence. Were you to pass from this earth, every one of you, we would remain, we would flourish, we would adapt. We would be shelter for the animals. We would purify the air even more. We would offer diversity, beauty and nurture. Our existence is not dependent upon you. You however are dependent upon us, for the air you breathe, for the food you eat, for the materials to build your shelters.

We are calling. It is time to bring your awareness and gratitude - listen, hear our voice. Demonstrate your gratitude, become responsible stewards; support yourselves, support us. Listen - we are calling.

Live mindfully, live and pay forward your appreciation. Listen and live.

The Voice of the Plant World

We nourish you.

We replenish you.

We strengthen you.
We rebuild you.
Each of us has a different meaningful existence
Just like yours
With a mission
With a purpose
With fulfillment

Each of our plant species has special uses
Medicinal, Nourishing, Healing, Cleansing
Some of us grow wild, some in your garden, cultivated

Some of us are feeding the animal kingdom,
Some the human kingdom
Some of us feed other plants
And most of us are here
To support a higher civilization, called the bees

We can go dormant for many years and keep within us
The sprouting seed once conditions change
We can be proliferate and provide you
With oxygen, with minerals, with nutrients
We can adapt to many changes and withstand
Fires, drought, storms and floods

We are an expression of variety
We are a symbol for and of life
We are an extension of wilderness
We are the voice of Mother Earth
And record keepers of knowledge and ancient wisdom

The more you value us
The more of this knowledge and ancient wisdom
You absorb
As the possibility of osmosis has no limit

Much can be learned from us
Through observation and meditation
We waste nothing and transform everything
This is how Abundance comes about
Deep within
We hold secrets of frequencies and vibrations
And those require stillness and an open heart
To hear
How the Great Mother Speaks

We welcome you always.
We are here in service,
With gratitude
And symbiosis
To learn and teach
And join in the circle
Of rejoicing in the cycle

Chapter 5

The Voice of the Woods

The voice of the woods is whispering - "YOU do not see the forest for the trees! I am enveloping, surrounding, embracing deep and mysterious. I am alive."

The woods/forests are not the trees, either individually or collectively. The Voice of the Woods was not a single voice, it is a choir.

The woods are more than their tall tree guardians. The woods are a collective voice: the alto of the great trees, the bells of the tiny bleeding hearts, hellebores and wild lilies, the graceful notes of the ferns, and the sustaining chorus of the berries and flowering shrubs.

The woods began to sing: The melodies of all the parts forming an earthly choir; a heavenly community right here on earth.

The voice of the woods is not a single voice. The woods speak of community, the trees stretch for the light, a light that we the human family also stretch to reach. The delicate plants, the shrubs are the covering and decoration, as we cover and adorn ourselves with clothes and jewelry. The earth itself is the foundation as our body is our foundation, the home of our soul. Hidden among and under are the animals: from the tiniest of insects to the graceful mountain lion and lynx, to the powerful and majestic bears and elk. The forest is truly a community: The forest embodies unity in diversity. It's voice a choir of celebration. The Voice of the Woods sings to us of what is possible when we live in harmony, when we grow in concert. When we open ourselves to the diversity that is.

The Voice of the Woods

I have been patiently waiting for you
To hear my voice
Yes, all living beings have consciousness
Finding the silence - you can hear us
Offering connection
Offering grounding
Offering clean air
And the wisdom of the ancients

Begin with a walk in the woods
Water a tree in the garden
Observe the willow's grace as her
Branches swing with the wind
Find the Oak's wisdom and rest in her shadow
Lean against a Redwood tree
And listen to what she has to tell you
From Ages ago

Each specimen is different in
Their offerings and yet
Each is my voice
The GREAT MOTHER SPEAKS
Through each of her children
As an individual
As a collective
This Voice will guide you
With Love and Wisdom
Unaltered, Unobstructed

Each tree, each plant, each flower
They all have needs which represent Your needs
Which reflect a part of you
That you can learn to nurture and grow

And plant and harvest
And love and cultivate
And enjoy and honor
And most of all respect

Respecting each other
Respecting yourself
From deep within
From the depth of each soul
Until each root touches another
And the web of our identity
Our rootedness
Our steadfastness
Our belonging
Becomes our true ONENESS
Not moving for hundreds of years
Teaches you patience.

Teaches that everything has its seasons
Of growth and expansion,
Of ripening and being fruitful,
Of the harvest depending on the effort and circumstances.

You put into yourself
Of the time period that seems like rest
And really is so much more

The illumination and creation of creativity
That seems asleep
And is ready to break through the wall of darkness
When the Light returns
Ready for a new start
Much can be gained from a retreat
Of always needing to bloom

Come join me in the circle of the ancestors
Who are inviting you in their many forms,
Into the heart of the connection of Earth
Of the workings beyond that which can be seen
The Un-manifest
That you sense in the presence of my voice
In the woods

I AM the Great Mother who speaks

Chapter 6

The Voice of the Animals

Our voices are many: We whisper, we shout, we are created in the bodies of the large, the small and the microscopic. We know you: Your tendency to focus upon the voices of the visible and the beautiful: the horse, the lion, the whale, the elephant, and the butterfly. It is easy for you to listen to beauty, to grace, to power.

Are you listening as closely to all our other voices? The voices of the invisible like the beneficial bacteria: the grubs, the earthworms, the gnats and the flies. Truly we embody the universal principle that everything has a right to exist: The beautiful, the "ugly", the powerful and the weak. Our voice is the voice of interconnectedness. Like our sister and brother plants and trees we are a community - an interdependent, interconnected community. As you listen, listen to the whisper as well as the shout. Listen for the seeming silence in between.

We have a message for you. Vitality and health is found in our diversity. As you damage our habitats so that we may not move freely and are challenged to find shelter and food you interrupt the ever present ebb and flow of how we support and interact with each other.

Listen to our voices. Your actions are silencing our voices: one at a time: One day soon the snow leopard's voice will only be found in a zoo.

Even now the black rhinoceros only sings in a game park. Each day some of our voices disappear, forever. Each day our collective voice; of the great, the tiny, the graceful and the invisible. Soon the only voices of ours that you will hear will be on a farm, or in a zoo or in your home.

Is that the future you desire to leave to the future generations?

With you choices, with your service, support us. Allow our full and diverse voice - to sing for you.

The Voice of the Animals

The Great Mother speaks
Through all the winged ones
The crawlers with many feet
The ones that swim in the rivers and oceans
The four-leggeds and the two-leggeds
Who roam free and wild
The ones domesticated and
Being animal companions
Wise beings as such

Their sounds are all different
Small and large
Still or Noisy
Faint or close by
Connected through ONE HEART
I express myself through all of creation

Connect with a lion and you will find
The gentleness underneath all his strength
The caring about the family bond
No different than the human kind
Strength and wisdom combined
With power and confidence
Medicine for anyone who he comes in contact with.

The elephant with wisdom and the capacity within
To remember in detail all she has ever experienced
And come from a place in the heart
That lets her soul be known and shine.

The tiger being feared, as being wild and free,
Has tactics and strategies
Anyone could wish to learn from

Without hesitation
Without blame or shame.
In his essence a master to
Respect and honor.

The birds of the jungle, the desert, the ocean
Far and wide

Each with his own song
And ability to see and have a vision
From the eagle's eye to reach a higher perspective
To share the gifts of joy and ease with us.

The horse in its original state of being
Is the purest of all beings
With strong leadership and
Survival instincts
Kind and authentic

Never aggressive unless threatened
Of service to the world and humanity.

Last but not least the dolphins and whales,
As representatives of an ever evolving civilization
Of high beings
With the ability to communicate through sound frequencies
To Heal and raise vibration
Empathic and telepathic.
They have the mission of helping humankind to evolve
Through Playfulness and Liberation
On all levels.

These are the animal representatives that have chosen to
Share their abilities and yet,
All animals have similar traits
And all are part of the circle of life.

A circle that is like the web of the spider connected to each and every one
No higher or lesser attributes than any other living organism
On this beautiful planet Earth,
Another expression of the Voice of the Great Mother.

Chapter 7

The Voice of the Mountains

I am the witness. I rose up from the skin of Mother Earth. I am literally her insides, brought outside. The invisible made visible.

I bring with me on this journey from the inside to the outside, great wealth in minerals and precious gems. Many of us have been here for millions of years. We have seen incredible transformations: the first animals crawling up out of the sea, the dramatic disappearance of whole races of animals. Hear me, I am the witness!

The Voice of the Mountains speaks of change, both instant and as slow and interminable as to feel timeless and changeless. In your brief time here as humans it can seem as if we are eternal and unchanging. Yet we are not.

We speak. We whisper. We speak to you of patience. We bear witness to times beyond your own memories. We speak to you of the illusion of barriers for there are passes through the highest and most formidable of us. We speak to you of the importance of being firmly anchored and reaching for the stars.

We speak of the certainty of change. We speak to you of endurance and strength

We speak to you.

The Voice of the Mountains

Glistening in the evening sunlight
Lays the mountainside
With its many colors
Of orange, yellow, green and grey.
Trees and rocks, open meadows
Rivers, streams
Life in abundance
All flowing from the rocks that were here
Long, long, long ago.

Before the floods
Before the oceans were divided
Before time was counted in years and days
And time became a concept.

The mountains listen
To thunder and lightning
The echoing of voices in the canyons
To the rain and snow
And the roaring of the mountain lion.

Unmoved for millennia
Witnessing history
Giving shelter to many
Being an obstacle to cross for some
Hardships and flourishing industries
Like a dance interwoven through history.

Be still and listen for yourself
I AM the Great Mother who you came to know
As the voice of the mountain.
The seeker of Truth
That you are

Searching for stillness
And longing for a place untouched by human
Hand and consciousness.
Wild and rocky
Flourishing and just
A peace of heaven
As close as it gets.
Come find the cave and rest
As long as troubles persist
To occupy your mind.

Find your way back into the world
When the Stillness is in you
I have become you
I AM with you.

Chapter 8

The Voice of the Desert

I AM the vastness and the ocean of sky that stretches to the horizon. No life seems to be apparent, dead I seem. Hot in the summer and during the day and cold in the winter and during the night.

Appearances tell you that extremes prevent life from flourishing here. When you sink into the silence and you sit in one spot you will find that you can hear me:

The little lizard appears from under a rock, a snake slithering along in the moonlight. Even the stars seem closer, almost reachable: Silence, no need for words. Communication happens without words. A bird of prey circles high above. He lends his eyes and vision to those who know how to tune in and become the seer. Higher and higher he circles until we become ONE. We are ONE.

The Voice of the Desert

What do men hear, when they come to me?
What do men see when they come into the heart of me?

Jesus came to me
Shamans come to me.
Within my heart
Prophets seek purification
Visions
Enlightenment.

Do you ever wonder
Why do they seek this from me
And not the city,
The lush countryside,
The abundant fields?

Have you ever beheld
Me
And thought
What a barren
Inhospitable place?

Open your eyes,
Life is all around.
In the heart of me you find
The line between life and death
Is very, very fine.

Rest with me awhile
You will discover life
Reduced to the most elemental.

The sand, the wind and the sun
They take away all that is not
Absolutely necessary.

Rest awhile with me
You will experience the vastness
And the silence of the night sky
And then you will hear
My voice
Whispering
"Look"!
"Look for God
He is hiding here
In plain sight."

Jesus found him,
The shamans found him
You too can find him.
Open your eyes,
Listen with your heart
And I will whisper the secret
Of life and God.

Chapter 9

The Voice of the Earth

Dear Children:

I am calling to you, whispering really; inviting you to join with me, inviting you to become a conscious part of this choir, my choir. Join your voice with my other voices and become a conscious connected part of my abundant and beauty filled home. Often I have noticed that you seem to separate yourself from my other voices - talking and moving upon and within me as if I am here for solely for your convenience. As if all my voices existed only to serve you. As if you were living in a motel instead of a home. If I was to describe your voice, it would be that you claimed the role as the star and solo headliner of our "show": A role that was never advertised, desired or written for you.

My voices, first and foremost - we are a choir.

All our voices are important to our song. There are times when one sings louder, more sweetly. There are times when the other voices quiet so that our total awareness may focus upon one particular voice, one particular song. The secret of our song, the power of its message is that we all, in our songs, celebrate the interconnectedness that our choir offers up in celebration.

You my child have grown more and more disruptive in your single-minded pursuit of what works for you. You are coming to a time dear child when the choir will begin to sing - a different song. We will all still be interconnected. Your perception, that our voices, only exist to serve you, that our presence or absence makes no difference to you- is creating a shift in the paradigm of interconnectedness and interdependence. I call on you, child of my body, child of my heart. Your choir misses you, your mother misses you. Your voice in full participation is the final part in the offering of our song of unity and creation.

Come join us in conscious awareness with a voice of moral authority, to add your voice to ours in celebration of the perfection of connection that life on me and within me is.

The Voice of Earth

Trust, oh Children of Earth
That all is provided for you:
Nourishment,
Abundance,
Health,
A place to call home.

The veins of my body deliver
All that you require to live;
Water, oxygen, food and shelter.
What is required of you is
Gratitude and
Recognition of Sacredness
In all aspects of life

Live it, love it and breathe it.
Do not take for granted even the smallest
Of signs and gestures that you get from many
Different sources to remember ME.

The sounds of the birds in the trees.
A groundhog's whistle
The whisper of the wind
The beats of hooves on the ground
The silent movement of the snake
Slithering towards a hiding spot
The bat that reminds you of confident movement
Through darkness and finding your way
The wild cat's courage, strength and focus
To remind you of your own vulnerability

Ancient species of turtles and elephants
Whales and dolphins and sharks
All here for a purpose

And with each species' extinction you lose something of yourself
An essence that is recognizable only
In its form of reflection of you

Once it is gone, it will be gone forever.
Each extinction far beyond the extent
You realize now.

Don't meddle with nature and think
You know better than creation itself!
Humble yourself!

Respect,
Bless,
Celebrate,
And hold dear
The meeting of souls through the eyes
And the heart of anyone you connect with.

Respect each being you meet.
See the essence of each soul.
See the essence of Mother Earth's soul,
The loving being I AM,
The womb of ultimate safety I provide.
The Beauty you recognize in each flower and tree
My creation as I bring forth life.
With each breath, with each turn, with each beat
Our hearts connected at the core
Providing steadiness
And the blessing of the Law of One

Take nothing for granted!
Once you start recognizing the balance of Life
You will stop destroying
And plundering
And killing
You will stop creating the Ego and feed it
With gadgets and ideas of the mind.

Humble yourself,
Recognize sacredness in the smallest ant
Building a hill.

The busiest bee
teaching a frequency and
Working for the survival of the whole.

Far beyond that of human existence
In a society that needs each of you.

Give thanks to the blessings that have been
bestowed upon you.
Humble yourself before the Creator
That you may live in peace and harmony.

Chapter 10

The Voice of the Wind

You see proof of me, in the dancing leaves. You feel my gentleness, as my invisible fingers caress your face. You see testimony of my power as the dark ominous funnel of the tornado announces my arrival. You see me in towering mountains of water and torrential rains as I sweep across the oceans as a hurricane or typhoon. I move the clouds from place to place; you can smell the coming rain in my breath. I am the gentlest of whispers and the warriors scream as he joins the fight. I rage, I play, I dance, I sway. Birds soar upon my invisible breath; trees are uprooted with my warrior's scream.

I am the Wind. I am the moving energetic manifestation of the earth's breath. I am not on the earth, yet I am born of the earth. I am necessary for life: I bring the rain; I carry the pollen and the seeds to spread their gifts across the face of the Mother. I bring the fragrance of the desert sage, the dampness of the forest floor, the ancient rose, and the exotic spices.

I offer to you, with my breath, free, non-polluting energy to create light for your homes and cities. You may channel my energy yet, it is not yours. You may feel me, yet you cannot hold me.

Truly of all the voices, I am the integrated voice of all you desire: kindness, abundance, power, and yes, children of the mother - I alone am the voice of freedom and change. I have many faces, yet my essence is the same.

Pay attention - learn from me. Own you essence, be flexible, and be responsive. Yet at your core remember, your existence you owe,

To our mother.

The Voice of the Wind

The Great Mother speaks in many forms,
whirlwinds, hurricanes, tornados,
the gentle light breeze
that moves the leaves of the trees on the mountain side
or the palm leaves by the ocean.

Measured in knots and strength
I move across the Great Plains, the deserts, the seas.
You have come to know my power,
the same power that resides within you.
All emotions, thoughts, intentions are moved by my voice-
the wind.

Let yourself be carried by me,
caressed by my gentleness,
reminded of your humbleness by my strength,

encouraged to move beyond any limitations
by the Eagle who rides on my wings.

Feel on your skin and within
the breath of the Universe,
that breathes you.
With each inhale
you become more of me,
I AM within you.

With each exhale
you give of yourself,
we are ONE.
Wind, breath, movement of air
connects you to the Great Spirit.

Listen closely as the wind speaks to you
- your reality shifts.
The wind becomes your prayer,
your breath is the entrance
to the door you have been looking for:
Silence:

The Silence of breath,
The Silence of mind.
Silence from longing and searching.
You have arrived.

I AM within you.

Chapter 11

Voice of the Living Masters

Of all the voices, this one is most insistent, most exacting. It is also the voice that hides- in plain sight. The distraction as we search for this voice is to focus upon the rich, the famous and the gurus: Mother Theresa, Nelson Mandela, Jimmy Carter, Ram Das, Stephen Covey, Wayne Dyer and Tony Robbins.

The Living Masters are an inner voice, whispering "you are missing US". You have missed what all living masters share. What unites us; what shines from us, is not our fame, our wealth, nor our role as a spiritual leader.

What unites us is our voice. For as living masters, we speak of many different things. We can be the humble collector of trash, a teacher of children, the leader of church or a person adding value by planting trees, aiding the frail or helping animals. We can be your plumber, your gardener. We can be sitting next to you in a theater, passing you on the street.

Who are we? How will you recognize us in all our different forms? You will recognize us by our voice. Whatever suit we wear, whatever we do in this life, our voices shares one common quality: Moral authority. We speak from that place of inner alignment of ethics, acts and thought. Our strength is quiet and clear. We all share an inner honesty and congruency.

Open your eyes, open your ears and open your heart. We are all around you. We wear many different suits and perform many different roles in society. Look not for some outer label of guru or spiritual leader. Look not for a messenger clothed in fame, in power, in beauty.

Look instead for integrity, consistency, honesty and integration of thought, action and heart. Look for strength and kindness. Look for confidence. Listen, for the moral authority that is present in everything we do, no matter what our role.

Be not distracted by our titles, our roles, our wealth or lack of it. Jesus was a carpenter, Buddha was a prince, and Mohammed was a merchant. Mother Theresa was a nun, Jimmy Carter was a president, Fernando is your gardener and your friend Ron was an ex-convict. Be not blinded by fame and brilliance. Listen and you will recognize us. Listen for the music of moral authority. That is our voice.

The Voice of the Living Masters

Simplicity in all you do
With a heart of Wisdom
A mind of Integrity
A compass of Honesty and Truth
Keeps the pendulum in balance

Not swinging to one extreme or another
Will get you gracefully to your goal
In all endeavors
Be kind

Know, that with each wonder and experience
You stretch and grow a little.
Stay humble and respectful
Grateful and truthful to your own path.
Keeping an open mind and an open heart
To learn from everyone.
The gift is to recognize the lesson.

Meditate and begin your transformation
As you find the balance and center.
To be quiet and still
Is to be rich and wealthy
With an inner life that no one can take
That no one can replace through words and
Teachings of any kind.

When you meet the Masters who have
The knowledge to stop the cycle of
Birth and death
Learn and ask for their blessings
So that you may gain this knowledge
Through initiations and transformations
That you can't read in any book

Walk this path called Life
In other people's shoes from time to time
So you may stay compassionate
And gain inner wisdom

About your own life choices
By looking at yourself
From an outside perspective.

Most of all stay child-like.
Stay with an open heart
With radiant joy
Enthusiasm, passion and love
For all you do and touch.
As each mission grows brighter
With the qualities you attribute to them.

Keep it simple!
As in simplicity you find much truth.
Keep your wonder and glance at the
Night sky and see the millions of
Twinkling lights.
Appreciate beauty
Of all that surrounds you and
Reflects your attitude about the world
Right back at you.
Keep your love for adventure
And exploration
To innovate and create anew.
Mostly be happy
In all you do.

We are here to walk the path alongside you.
Ask for our guidance and help and we
Will be there to assist.
Any day
And moment in time.

PART II

The Call to Action

After having journeyed the different voices of nature expressed through the animals, nature, the elements, the living Masters and Mother Earth herself we felt a strong call to action. We did research to find tools to support earth, the Great Mother. We decided to offer some of these tools as suggested pragmatic and do-able guidelines for those willing to step up with simple actions in ways that support the world they desire to leave as a legacy for future generations.

These suggestions and resources are a beginning - they are pragmatic, doable right now with no preparation, no "investment". Consider the suggestions that follow as a journey, taken one step at a time - to support the earth and create a legacy for future generations, one choice at a time.

Chapter 1

Let's Move From the Blame Game to the Quick Fix

To paraphrase Oscar Wilde

"WE KNOW THE PRICE OF EVERYTHING AND THE COST OF NOTHING."

We know the price of each six pack of bottled water, each pound of organic versus grass fed versus regular meat, organic versus regular vegetables yet we do not know the cost of each of those choices. Beyond the price tag, what is the cost to the earth, the environment, our health, our ethics, and the welfare of animals? What government subsidies are paid to subsidize cheap prices? Your regular factory farmed chicken may be fed with corn the price of which is supported by government subsidies, by tax breaks for the factory farm, by non-union labor. Then the real cost of meat, of commodities such as oil, gas, corn, wheat is being absorbed through the payments of your tax dollars. So the chicken when sells to you for $1.19 per pound may be receiving the equivalent of $2.00 to $4.00 per pound in government subsidies and tax benefits: its price is $1.19

per pound, its monetary cost is closer to 3.19 to $5.19 per pound. You think it is cheap when in fact part of the cost of your choice is paid by every other tax payer. Additionally the subsidies and tax breaks that create these lower cost commodities support the widespread use of oil, of factory farms, of monoculture farming. When we know this, will we make different choices or will we choose to continue with what is familiar and let future generations resolve the challenges that result from our choices?

Do you hear yourself saying yes the environment is important, but I am just one person? This is the voice of powerlessness, victimization and abdication of responsibility. It is easier to "pass the buck". This is a problem for the government to take up. Laws have to be changed etc. Well we invite you to change the story you are telling yourself about how powerless you are to be a positive change in the world. Almost every environmental abuse, mistreatment of workers and exploitation of animals is the direct result of the search for even more profits and or the control of natural resources. History shows us that individual consumer awareness and choice can change business practices and contribute to creating the change we desire to see in the world. As Harry Truman, 33rd president of the United States said: "the buck stops here", it stops with you!, with us! No excuses.

This section of the Voice of the "Great Mother" takes issues and offers simple, immediate personal actions that you can take to create change. The question to ask instead of is it possible to make a change? IS "am I willing to?" Are you willing to quit "passing the buck" quit making excuses and be part of the solution?

Buying Bottled Water

To use or not use bottled water offers us the opportunity to expand our awareness about how the universal laws of cause and effect and incremental effect interact in our daily choices. This choice is truly micro input, macro output.

Most bottled water is either tap water run through a reverse osmosis system and then put into plastic bottles for resale, OR it is water from springs and aquifers, which are tapped by companies such as Coca Cola or Nestlé. These companies buy the sources of natural pure water, bottle it and then market it nationwide and worldwide. The implications to consider are those experienced by California. For one example: Nestlé has a contract with an Indian reservation in the high desert of Southern California. It has purchased the rights to draw water from this aquifer for use by its Arrowhead bottling plant. This aquifer is also used by surrounding communities and farms. In times of drought, the aquifer is being diminished faster than it can be replaced and the water is being sold like a renewable commodity endangering the surrounding communities' ability to tap into this local water for the personal and agricultural uses of the community and the state. It is one thing to purchase bottled water when you do not have access to safe drinking water. It is another thing to purchase this bottled water when you have sources of safe drinking water readily available in your community, within your home. When we purchase bottled water, we are responding out of habit, from the influence of advertising. We can change this instantly.

What Can You Do?

Instead of purchasing bottled water, make a onetime purchase of a water bottle that is BPA free. Then refill this bottle as you require.

With this choice you are instantly making a change, supporting the environment, keeping water usage local instead of supporting its sale like a commodity such as Gator Aide or Coke. This choice removes the production and disposal of plastic from the environment. This choice keeps your water consumption local. You can, by this conscious choice, support the earth, become more mindful and make a difference.

Different Ways to Source Your Drinking Water

Get a Water Filter for Your House

One solution for those who feel tap water is not as safe or supportive of optimum health is to install your own water filter system in some form. It can be a Britta water container that contains its own filter, sits on the kitchen sink and is easily refillable. You can select an under the counter reverse osmosis system. This is more expensive and the filter units usually have to be replaced every one to two years. The challenge here is to remember to replace the filters.

Use a Water Cooler/Reverse Osmosis Water

You can contract with a local source of spring water, or a water store that will supply you with a cooler and water. The water from water stores is reverse osmosis water produced in the store from regular local tap water. The advantage of this system is that you only pay for the water you use and you replenish it as needed. The disadvantage is that you are required to participate by traveling to the water store, filling the bottles and then returning them home. You can use containers that vary in size from 1 gallon to 5 gallon.

The water delivered to your home is usually sourced from a spring. Here the opportunity is to only purchase water from a spring in your area. This aligns consumption with the people living in the area. It reduces the use of plastic, oil and gas to transport packaged product. When the water is delivered to you the advantage is convenience. However you must still bring the water in and lift it up onto the coolers. The disadvantage is often the delivery system does not align with your personal consumption. Either bringing the water before you desire it, or you running out before the next delivery date

Reduce Pollution of Plastic Containers

The rise in the use of bottled water, the increased cost of fuel and shipping has resulted in a dramatic rise in the use of plastic containers for shelf items in stores, for bottled water. While many communities and environmentally conscious people participate in local recycling there continues to be a huge number of plastic containers that end up in our oceans, littering our deserts, forests and roadsides.

Buy Products in Glass Containers

Consider buying glass bottles and products in glass rather than in plastic or metal. First of all it is healthier as glass doesn't give of toxicity as plastic and metal do[1]. Try kinesiology when you are in the store and see what is better for you!

[1] http://www.scientificamerican.com/article/plastic-not-so-fantastic/

Glass containers and bottles can also be reused and if not they can be recycled far easier than plastic and metal. First think: Can I avoid the trash or byproduct all together, which would be best, of course. If that is not possible then what happens to the trash once I have used the product itself? Avoid plastic and instead store your things in glass or pottery in the fridge or when you store things rather than using plastic ware or such. It is so much healthier for the planet and healthier for you and your family!

BUY LOCAL – 50 MILE RADIUS

When you buy groceries: First GO LOCAL, then go ORGANIC. Of course, organic is great but if it is shipped from thousands of miles across the world to get to you it might have accumulated radiation, travel residues, and contributed even more of a carbon footprint because of traveling great distances by air, ship, truck or train. Additionally most countries do not have the same standards of inspection and certification requirements for organic certification that are present in the U.S.

When you make this choice you are supporting small local farmers and growers around you: individuals that you can have a relationship with, that will tell you how they go about their operations, which soil the product is grown in, how conscious are they themselves. We believe that when you grow things with love it nourishes our bodies even more! You keep the mom and pop stores in business rather than giving your money to big chains and corporations that are getting the upper hand of the market and dictate the rules of market prices, regulations, FDA approval etc.

Support Your Co-Op Around The Corner, Or The Farmer's Market

The little vegetable stand on the corner has their field just outside of town. It will be fresher and healthier for you to eat what grows around you. This is how nature intended it to be! Of course, if you live in the desert and you are craving bananas you have to ship that, right? But it is about growing your awareness and consciousness and to make the choices with each product you buy to contribute to supporting the world, health for your body and for the environment. So we are not saying Never buy this or that. What we are saying is to become aware and conscious how you contribute to the bigger picture with your OWN VOICE that is reflected in how and what you consume.

Go Vegetarian 1-2x Per Week Or More

We have a world population of about 7 billion people on this planet: Growing by about 200,000 each day. The poorer countries currently consume very little meat. Meat is cheap and available in developed countries because we have government subsidies and tax systems that support factory farming. Factory farming is an euphemism for raising animals in very crowed, unnatural conditions and feeding them steroids, GMO feed and antibiotics to encourage rapid growth and to prevent the disease that is a natural outcome of living in these unnatural and overcrowded conditions. When you purchase this inexpensive, factory farmed meat you are supporting this inhumane treatment of animals and you are taking into your own bodies the meat of animals that are fed growth hormones, steroids and antibiotics. This is in fact becoming a huge health issue and is suspected of contributing to the rise of antibiotic resistant bacteria. We simply don't have the land to have all of the factory farm animals on free range, nor do we have the resources to produce healthy animals[1]

What Can You Do?

Find recipes that are meat and fish free. Change your habit of going into the store and steering towards the meat and dairy section first and instead choose the vegetable and fruit section first. See vegetables and plant-based products as the MAIN thing on your plate. Start thinking differently! It will have a huge effect on how you shop, how you live and what you value.

You will discover a whole new range of possibilities of how you can nourish your body and keep it healthy and even healthier without the consumption or at least a reduced consumption of meat, fish and possibly even without dairy.

Choose to create meatless days 1-2x per week or more. Every meal that you choose to prepare vegetarian, is a meal that supports health and does not contribute to inhumane animal raising practices. When you do choose to eat meat, buy organic and local when possible.

Imagine also with each animal that is killed what tremendous suffering you take into your own body. The hormones of stress and pain are in the meat, no matter how we would like that to not be this way and close our eyes to this fact. You are literally consuming stress and pain and then wonder why you are stressed out and why you have certain symptoms in your body that you seem to not be able to explain? Cut back on meat, fish and dairy and see what happens!

Consider vegan

As we began to write this section, we experienced very strong resistance to including information about several very common practices to the factory farming of food products derived from animals. We did not want to believe these statements so we began to research and to our surprise this is what we found.

Egg Industry

Chick Culling: This includes practices in which unwanted male chicks that are unnecessary in the production of eggs are slaughtered. One of the methods, actually considered the most humane is to grind them up alive since death is instanteous[2]

[1] Cowspiracy: The Sustainability Secret 2014- Directed by Kip Andersen, Keegan Kuhn.

[2] Wikipedia: Chick Culling

In many states the chickens are kept in small cages where they are not able to turn around, stand up etc. California enacted, by public referendum, new laws to ensure that chickens were raised with more space. The predictions that the eggs would become so expensive that ordinary people could not afford them have not proven to be true.

What can you do?

Buy your eggs from local small producers. Buy organic, buy cage free. To be clear none of these practices eliminate the practice of chick culling. What they do promote is more humane and healthy conditions for the chickens that produce eggs.

Dairy Industry

The most significant instances of animal abuse occur in factory farming of all types. Even some "organic" producers have been investigated for practices that are not aligned with guidelines for humane treatment.

Here are a couple of links where you can read current information on factory farming, the implications for human health, animal welfare and basic decency.

http://www.peta.org/issues/animals-used-
for-food/animals-used-food-factsheets/
veal-byproduct-cruel-dairyindustry

http://www.alternet.org/story/145378/
got milk a disturbing look at the dairy industry

The short version is ALL dairy products: milk, sour cream, cottage cheese, cheese, ice cream that are produced through factory farming practices are to be avoided if you have any regard for the humane treatment of animals.

What Can You Do?

Use dairy alternatives such as soy milk, rice milk, coconut milk or almond milk. Look for the words pasture raised, no growth hormones, no antibiotics and vegetarian feed? After doing this research we are making even more changes in the food that we eat and are consciously choosing to reduce or eliminate the intake of cheese and other dairy products or to only consume pasture raised dairy products that are also organic.

Meat Production

Simply put, much of our land, water and air resources go to support the raising of animals for food. Additionally while developed countries have the highest consumption of meat per person, they also consume the most beef, which is the least efficient in the conversion of food taken in to amount of meat produced. Of all forms of meat available chicken and pork are the easiest on the environment and consume the least amount of feed for pounds of meat produced.

For a more detailed exploration of the implications of raising animals for human food please follow the links below.

http//science.time.com/2013/12/16/the-triple-whopper-environmental-impact-of-global-meat-production/

https://en.wikipedia.org/wiki/Environmental_impact_of_meat_production

It is a common belief that you have to have animal protein to live healthy and get all the nutrition you need. Other studies have shown that animal products are a huge cause of tumor growth/cancer and that societies who do not eat animal products all together do not have these issues. Below are two links that you can follow to make up your own mind about whether to do one or more of the following:

http://www.scientificamerican.com/article/should-humans-eat-meat-excerpt/

http://www.pcrm.org/health/diets/vegdiets/how-can-i-get-enough-protein-the-protein-myth

What Can You Do?

1. Choose to reduce your consumption of meat. Dedicate 2 or more days per week, or 12 or more meals per week to being meatless

2. Choose to create a vegetarian diet for you and your family

3. Choose to embrace a vegan diet, which would mean absolutely no products from animals. If not fully vegan choices then even a partial vegan life style would make a huge difference! We encourage you to give it a thought. There are many resources out there to help you make this change and transition to a vegan life style.

4. Buy Organic
    When you commit to buying organic vegetables, fruit and meat you are usually supporting small family farms and individual enterprise instead of corporations. This is, however, changing as large supermarket chains now market organic products from "their own farms" Buying organic as a way to support the environment, decrease the use of pesticides, and promote wise stewardship of the land is most effective when it is coupled with buy local. For a detailed discussion of this read Michael Pollan's book: The Omnivore's Dilemma. This book can support you to become even more aware about the ways in which your food choices can change the entire food industry. For example when you buy organic grapes grown in Chile, the impact on the environment because of the transportation

carbon footprint is so high, you can support the environment with an even better choice by buying local or buying no pesticides but not organic AND buying in season.

5. Buy Meat – Grass Fed/No Antibiotics/No Hormones
   Buying grass fed/no hormones and no antibiotic and vegetarian fed meat is intimately connected with the previous two entries: buy local and buy organic. When you choose to eat meat in any form, be mindful about how it is raised, how it is transported, how it is "slaughtered". Each point in this journey of farm to table is an opportunity to support the earth, and make even more mindful and ethical choices aligned with your own personal values. Each point is an opportunity to create a ritual of awareness, consciousness and gratitude as you chose the food for yourself and your family.

Other Things You Can Do

Use Led Light Bulbs

One of the easiest ways to reduce your use of electricity and thereby save money and thereby use less energy is to replace all incandescent light bulbs with LED's OR with the very long lived lower wattage versions of some new incandescent bulbs. Here is a website that can support you to understand the difference, and learn how to create equivalents from incandescent to LED:

http://globalnews.ca/news/539681/
what-you-need-to-know-about-led-bulbs/

Even though this article was written with Canadian references, the discussion of why the switch to LED lights is important remains valid. Remember that regardless, the lower the wattage, the dimmer the light.

Purchase Energy Efficient Appliances

In recent years, new appliances have become even more energy efficient. Energy efficiency in appliances has been driven my government regulations requiring standards to be set and reviewed for a number of appliances:

An example of energy savings through appliance and equipment standards is the refrigerator. A new refrigerator today uses a third of the energy it did in 1973, but offers 20% more storage capacity and costs half as much. Other efficiency gains in household appliances since 1990 include:

New clothes washers use 70% less energy

New dishwashers use 40% less energy

New air conditioners use 50% less energy

New furnaces use 10% less energy

As your appliances require replacement consider looking at their Energy Star rating. This will save you money each and every year and contribute to energy conservation and environmental protection.

Here is an informative website regarding the history of the development of energy efficient appliances. http://energy.gov/eere/buildings/history-and-impacts

Gas Efficient Cars

(http://energyalmanac.ca.gov/gasoline/
gasoline_cpi_adjusted.html) As you consider your next car,
instead of 20 or 30mpg, day after day, week after week, year
after year imagine averaging 44 miles per gallon, year after
year: Over the years such a car more than pays for itself.
Consider leaving your stories about what you need; your ego's
desire to look cool, sexy and successful and pick a car/vehicle
that is kinder of the environment, either a hybrid, electric
or high mpg vehicle. When you do this you contribute to
reducing the demand for fossil fuels, contributing to cleaner
air, lessening the influence of advertising, and aligning your
personal purchases with your values.

Drive Less/More Efficiently

One of the great lessons to be learned from driving a hybrid
car is taught by its' on board computer that showed how
the car is using fuel. When the hybrid engine engaged,
how the fuel consumption increased dramatically when you
accelerate or drive the car faster: even 5-10 mph faster. This
little computer can support you to become a more aware and
conscious driver. The other thing you can do may be a bit
out of your comfort zone however it is worth it. Consider
carpooling, or ride sharing to events and or driving between
55-60mph. As your driving speed is reduced there is an
interesting side benefit. You become even more relaxed.
Driving during traffic hours, caught in traffic jams relax
into the experience. Driving 10-20 mph over the speed limit

will save you 10 minutes and potentially cost you several hundred dollars. Relax into the experience and driving becomes even more enjoyable, no matter the speed.

Grow Your Own Vegetables in Pots, Raised Beds

If you have the space in your garden or even in the house you could grow your vegetables in pots or raised beds and redesign your lawns to food producing spaces that need just as much water as a green lawn does. You can mulch to keep the water usage down. This encourages and deepens your connection with the soil and plants and the food you take in. Think that every time you care about your tomato plants, veggies or lettuce and you give it loving thoughts you actually give this love to yourself as you and your family will be eating that nourishment you gave to the plant. It is a cycle of giving and receiving and sacred as such.

It takes some time to care for a garden but you could see it as the time you would be sitting in a car or bus and drive to the store and go shopping. The other advantage is that you know exactly what you give your plants, what soil you grow it in, you could even do a mineral analysis of your soil to know what might be lacking or what may need reducing, you know for sure you are going to grow it organically without pesticides or any other byproducts. You could start your own compost with compost worms that turn your left over plants into the most nourishing soil fertilizing in turn the food you grow. As you do this you will notice how in tune you get with each plant and the growing seasons, the moon cycles and when your plant is thirsty, needs some extra nutrients and so forth. It gets you in touch and in tune with the cycles of life even if you live in a city apartment. Please check out the amazing salad bar racks, which you can use to grow food in very small spaces...

Repair Instead of Replace

As a society we have gotten used to throwing things away and buying new appliances, computers, cell phones, tires, clothes, gadgets, the list is endless. But what if we repaired things and bought quality products rather than cheap products that are made to only last a certain amount of time. Think about how your grandparents brought things to a repairperson so things could be longer in use. This also kept small businesses alive and supported local people. The trash produced would be so much less! Sometimes, it doesn't make sense if you have a very old fridge that uses that much more electricity than a new one would; maybe it is time to replace that one. But in general, we could avoid a lot of trash by adopting the thinking if nothing is wrong with it, we should hold on to it and use it until it breaks or give it to a repurpose store (known as a thrift store) store for use for someone else instead of taking it to the landfill. Over the years our economy has become driven by consumer spending, which has resulted in consumer debt. It is as if our prosperity is built on a shifting foundation of sand. So instead of employing people to provide services and support quality of life by increasing we support the consumption of things. And therefore we have indirectly come to depend upon planned obsolescence.

Think also about what you buy. Will this product last? Can it actually be repaired? Or is there a similar product that gives us this choice of repair? A new cell phone, do we actually need the newest model or is the one we have still working and we can wait another year? Can I buy something second hand and contribute to reusing and repurposing and repairing something? I just bought an "antique" that is in need of repair of this and that but the quality of how it was made is better than anything that I could buy today and so it is worth repairing and fixing up and re-using! Another bonus is it has character and is loved, valued and one-of-a-kind.

Chapter II

Conclusion

As you hear the manifold voices of The Great Mother Speaks let your life be infused with ever growing awareness of the Oneness and the Web of Life that connects all of us — each being, human and animal, plant, mineral and rock and Mother Earth herself. Let your beliefs, doubts and justifications be surrendered to the love for this planet and all of Creation. Commit to one or more things you can change in your own life that contributes to a sustainable and harmonized dance here on Earth.

We have put together some resources that you can use, if you choose, to delve deeper into any of the subjects we have touched upon. The truth is simple, the concepts are simple and few words are needed. The implementation of Change is ours. It is up to each one of us to create an abundantly healthy world that will be here for our future generations. The vision we hold, with conviction is that Change is possible NOW. As we focus our intention upon the world we desire to see, so it will become.

As we began to collaborate and share in the journey that this book is, our individual voices, our individual ideas of what the Great Mother would say and who she is, began to be transformed as we became messengers of her voice instead of speakers sharing ideas about what her voice would say.

This same transformation from sharing our individual opinions to becoming messengers of the greater whole continued as we began to develop the section called the Call to Action. The Call to Action is an invitation, for every reader, to step into even more congruency. To align even more your words about commitment to health, commitment to the earth, love for animals and the truth of climate change with your personal choices and the way in which you "spend" your energy ie money. Are you willing to put your money where your mouth is? Are you willing to transform your words, your postings about kindness to animals, protection of the environment, etc into actions? Are you willing to make a change, let go of old habits, old patterns of living, eating, cooking and shopping?

In the process of contributing to the creation of this book, we actually experienced a shift from the little we of the two of us to a larger collective we. We wrote the book as an invitation to others to change. The gift was our own personal transformation in the process.

In the process of being agents of change, we were changed. This book is simple. The calls to action ask you what can you change right now: You personally, through your individual choices.

You are invited to say yes, to an opportunity to create change – NOW. There are no excuses, every action is possible and do-able.

Resources

Books:

The Relationship Of Man To His Food

Barstow, Cynthia; <u>The Eco-Foods Guide (What's Good for the Earth is Good for You)</u> Easy to read exploration of how to make your food choices in a way that best support the earth

Jones, Ellis; <u>The Better World Shopping Guide: Every Dollar Makes A Difference –</u> If you are going to have only one resource to support you to create change now- this is it. It is small, easy to carry, easy to use. Gives major brand products in every category a report card and a brief summary of which company is notable for. Has a great list of resources you can explore to obtain further information. This is one of our favorite books.

Pollan, Michael; <u>The Ominvores Dilema –</u> This is a relevant discussion of farm to table. Exploring the tradeoffs of buying organic, local, pesticide free. We found this book to offer a readable and intelligent discussion and exploration.

Creating A More Sustainable Life

Suzuki, David &Boyd, David R.; <u>David Suzuki's Green Guide</u> This is a practical "how to" book to support you to make greener choices and influence government

Hawken, Paul; Lovins, Amory; Lovins, Hunter L.: <u>Natural Capitalism</u> This is an in depth discussion of capitalism and the new revolution- corporations drawing their profits and being environmentally responsible at the same time. Provides detailed footnotes,

Videos

Julia Roberts as The Voice of Mother Nature-
<u>https://www.facebook.com/omeletocom/
videos/10153768659494494/?pnref=story</u>

Al Gore- The Inconvenient Truth

CONSIDER VEGETARIAN/VEGAN

Movies:

Cowspiracy: We found this movie very informative

Books:

T. Colin Campbell, Ph. D. and Thomas M. Campbell II, MD: <u>The China Study</u> This is another source that we found very informative

J. Morris Hicks: <u>Healthy Eating – Healthy World</u>

Peter Tompkins and Christopher Bird: <u>The Secret Life of Plants</u> (also as movie)

Pamphlets:

Cruelty FREE Shopping Guide from PETA: a small pocket guide to a list of companies that do not test their products on animals.

Seafood Watch.org: Seafood Watch- a small pocket guide to purchasing seafood that is harvested in an environmentally sensitive manner, seafood to avoid either do to overfishing or high levels of contaminants.

About Us

Linda Heller

29 years ago on a vision quest in the Coastal Mountains of Santa Barbara County Linda was shown her life purpose: Through the next 29 years, no matter what her outward vocation or professional title as a teacher, a life coach, a Certified Trainer of Transcendental Rebirthing, a credentialed teacher, a Certified Jinn Shin Jyutsu Practitioner a Certified Breath Worker (Conscious Connected Breathing) and she earned a Master's degree in education, the mission kept unfolding and kept manifesting. Her life purpose, no matter the position or title was one of service. During this journey she explored the traditions of the Native Americans and participated in vision quests, healing circles, ceremonial sweats and shamanic drumming circles. She met with the shamans/medicine men of the Hopis and the Chumash and supported their work and gatherings in her community. For many years Linda has lived flowing between these 3 worlds: the worlds of spirit, the world of energy and work.

Linda's entire professional and personal life has been a quest to manifest that integration of spirit, energy and service. In her own words, "Co-authoring the Great Mother Speaks was for me initially a way to share yet another part of myself: To integrate and share with others my commitment to the earth and to be a messenger of change and self-empowerment. In the process of co-authoring this book, I not only gave of myself, I received. I received a deepening awareness and realignment of my personal values and life choices."

Linda Heller
www.lindaheller.org
Linda Heller on Facebook
School for Sacred Ceremony on Facebook

Claudia Mardel

Claudia has always deeply loved nature and animals and the beauty that is reflected within each being. She has traveled and explored many cultures and religions and found herself drawn to the simplicity of life within the tribes of Africa, India, Tibet and North America finding much wisdom in the teachings these tribes preserve. She has studied many different religions and philosophies finding that Mother Earth has the simplest teachings, which ask us for respect, humbleness and gratitude and to see our life as a great blessing.

She studied to be able to translate the space and the voices of animals and other life forms, the Ascended Masters and those who have passed before us. Claudia is also teaching the art of communicating this way in her program Academy Of The Radiant Soul, facilitating online and live programs at Radiant Soul Sanctuary. She is helping others through transitions of different types, one of them being the transition at the moment of death in the Roadmap Home

Claudia is also a published author. You may find her autobiographical journey Where the Desert Meets the Cedar on amazon.com

Claudia is also honoring Mother Earth through her art forms of Pottery and Photography. Each creation pays tribute to the sacredness of life itself. As Claudia "creates" her pottery, each creation is an "intentional creation" filled with prayers for the person using or connecting with the piece of clay.

A passion for creation and celebration of connection fills all of Claudia's professional and creative work. As a potter, a photographer, an author and a life coach Claudia imbues everything she does and is with a celebration for the sacredness of life.

www.radiantsoul.org
www.roadmaphome.org
www.claudiamardel.com

Printed in the United States
By Bookmasters